Geochronologic and Geochemical Data from Mesozoic Rocks in the Black Mountain Area Northeast of Victorville, San Bernardino County, California

Open-File Report 2013–1146

U.S. Department of the Interior
U.S. Geological Survey

Cover: View east toward the Black Mountain limestone quarry northeast of Victorville, California, which is developed in limestone conglomerate of the Jurassic Fairview Valley Formation. Hills in distance are composed primarily of the Jurassic Sidewinder Volcanics. Photograph by Paul Stone, February 9, 2003.

Geochronologic and Geochemical Data from Mesozoic Rocks in the Black Mountain Area Northeast of Victorville, San Bernardino County, California

By Paul Stone, Andrew P. Barth, Joseph L. Wooden, Nicole K. Fohey-Breting, Jorge A. Vazquez , and Susan S. Priest

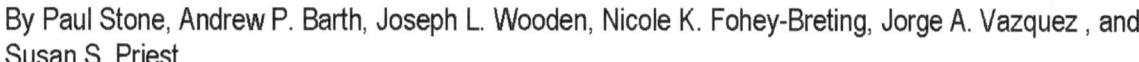

Open-File Report 2013–1146

U.S. Department of the Interior
U.S. Geological Survey

U.S. Department of the Interior
SALLY JEWELL, Secretary

U.S. Geological Survey
Suzette M. Kimball, Acting Director

U.S. Geological Survey, Reston, Virginia: 2013

For more information on the USGS—the Federal source for science about the Earth,
its natural and living resources, natural hazards, and the environment—visit
http://www.usgs.gov or call 1–888–ASK–USGS

For an overview of USGS information products, including maps, imagery, and publications,
visit *http://www.usgs.gov/pubprod*

Suggested citation:
Stone, P., Barth, A.P., Wooden, J.L., Fohey-Breting, N.K., Vazquez, J.A., and Priest, S.S., 2013,
Geochronologic and geochemical data from Mesozoic rocks in the Black Mountain area northeast of
Victorville, San Bernardino County, California: U.S. Geological Survey Open-File Report 2013–1146, 31
p.

Contents

Figures

Tables

Conversion Factors, Abbreviations, and Chemical Symbols

Conversion Factors

Multiply	By	To obtain
Length		
centimeter (cm)	0.3937	inch (in.)
millimeter (mm)	0.03937	inch (in.)
meter (m)	3.281	foot (ft)
kilometer (km)	0.6214	mile (mi)
kilometer (km)	0.5400	mile, nautical (nmi)
meter (m)	1.094	yard (yd)

Abbreviations

CL	Cathodoluminescence
Ma	Mega-annum (a unit of time equivalent to one million years)
ppm	parts per million
SHRIMP-RG	Sensitive High Resolution Ion Microprobe–Reverse Geometry
TAS	Total Alkali-Silica
XRF	X-Ray Fluorescence

Chemical Symbols

Al	Aluminum	Pb	Lead
Ba	Barium	Rb	Rubidium
Ca	Calcium	Si	Silicon
Fe	Iron	Sr	Strontium
K	Potassium	Th	Thorium
Mg	Magnesium	Ti	Titanium
Mn	Manganese	U	Uranium
Na	Sodium	Y	Yttrium
O	Oxygen	Zn	Zinc
P	Phosphorus	Zr	Zirconium

Geochronologic and Geochemical Data from Mesozoic Rocks in the Black Mountain Area Northeast of Victorville, San Bernardino County, California

By Paul Stone, Andrew P. Barth, Joseph L. Wooden, Nicole K. Fohey-Breting, Jorge A. Vazquez, and Susan S. Priest

Abstract

We present geochronologic and geochemical data for Mesozoic rocks in the Black Mountain area northeast of Victorville, California, to supplement previous geologic mapping. These data, together with previously published results, limit the depositional age of the sedimentary Fairview Valley Formation to Early Jurassic, refine the ages and chemical compositions of selected units in the overlying Jurassic Sidewinder Volcanics and of related intrusive units, and limit the age of some post-Sidewinder faulting in the Black Mountain area to a brief interval in the Late Jurassic. The new information contributes to a more complete understanding of the Mesozoic magmatic and tectonic evolution of the western Mojave Desert and surrounding regions.

Introduction

Mountain ranges in the vicinity of Victorville, California (fig. 1) contain extensive outcrops of volcanic, sedimentary, and plutonic rocks that hold important clues for reconstructing the Mesozoic paleogeographic and tectonic evolution of the western Mojave Desert. One significant outcrop area is centered around Black Mountain, 15 km northeast of Victorville, where two units of particular interest, the sedimentary Fairview Valley Formation and the overlying Sidewinder Volcanics, are well exposed. Several previous geologic mapping studies (Bowen, 1954; Dibblee, 1960, 1967; Stone, 1964; Miller, 1977, 1978, 1981) and topical investigations (Walker, 1985, 1987; Schermer, 1993; Schermer and Busby, 1994; Schermer and others, 2002; Fohey-Breting and others, 2010) have shown that rocks exposed at Black Mountain provide an unusually complete record of Triassic and Jurassic events in the Mojave Desert region. Structural complexities and insufficient geochronologic data in the area, however, have precluded a complete understanding of the geologic history.

Stone (2006) remapped the geology of the Black Mountain area primarily to clarify the stratigraphic and structural relations of the Fairview Valley Formation and Sidewinder Volcanics. During and after that study, several map units were sampled for uranium-lead (U-Pb) zircon geochronology and geochemical analysis. In this report, we present the resulting geochronologic and geochemical data to supplement the preliminary geologic map of Stone (2006).

Geologic Framework

The Black Mountain area (fig. 2) consists of Mesozoic and minor Paleozoic rocks (table 1) surrounded by alluvial deposits of late Cenozoic age. The area is transected by the Helendale Fault (Bowen, 1954; Miller and Morton, 1980; Aksoy, 1993), one of several late Cenozoic, northwest-striking, right-lateral faults that make up the Eastern California Shear Zone (Dokka and Travis, 1990; Petersen and Wesnousky, 1994; Sauber and others, 1994). This study focuses on the Fairview Valley Formation, Sidewinder Volcanics, and associated rocks exposed northeast of the Helendale Fault.

In this area (figs. 2 and 3), Paleozoic marble and calc-silicate rocks (units Pzm, Pzmc; fig. 4A) are intruded by late Early or early Middle Triassic monzonite (unit Trm) that Barth and Wooden (2006) dated as 244±2 Ma. These rocks are unconformably overlain by the Jurassic Fairview Valley Formation, which consists of a basal conglomeratic unit (Jfv$_1$; fig. 4B); a thick middle part (units Jfv$_2$, Jfv$_3$) composed of mudstone, siltstone, sandstone, conglomerate, and minor limestone (fig. 4C–E); and an upper part (units Jfv$_4$, Jfv$_5$) characterized by massive limestone conglomerate (fig. 4F). Geochronologic data (Stone and others, 2005; this report) indicate that the Fairview Valley Formation was deposited no earlier than about 194 Ma. The Fairview Valley Formation is largely homoclinal but is locally folded (figs. 2 and 5). A major syncline was mapped in the upper part of the Fairview Valley Formation by Bowen (1954), Dibblee (1960), and Stone (1964), but not by Miller (1977) or Stone (2006).

The Fairview Valley Formation is overlain by a thin, unnamed sequence of sedimentary rocks (units Jvc, Jslc, Jch, Jqs) mainly composed of conglomerate and sandstone. The basal contact of this sequence is an angular unconformity that cuts westward and down section across unit 5, unit 4, and the upper part of unit 3 of the Fairview Valley Formation (figs. 2 and 3). Angular relations across the unconformity indicate that the Fairview Valley Formation was tilted about 35° eastward before deposition of the overlying strata. The western exposed part of the unconformity is bent to a northwesterly trend, in general alignment with bedding in unit 3 of the Fairview Valley Formation. The strata just below this part of the unconformity, however, are complexly folded into an inverted antiform, and the unconformity itself appears to be overprinted by a fault that truncates the northeastern limb of this fold (fig. 2).

The quartz-rich sandstone (unit Jqs) that caps the thin sedimentary sequence is overlain by the oldest rocks of the Jurassic Sidewinder Volcanics ("northern sequence" of Stone, 2006) (figs. 2 and 3). The dominant unit (Jsnr) of this sequence, a rhyolitic ignimbrite (fig. 4G) that Schermer and Busby (1994) called the tuff of Black Mountain, was dated as late Early Jurassic (181±3 Ma) by Fohey-Breting and others (2010). The upper part of the northern sequence includes feldspathic sandstone and conglomerate (unit Jsns), quartzose sandstone (unit Jsnq), and finely laminated volcanic rocks (unit Jsnl) distinct from the rhyolitic ignimbrite (table 1). Bodies of intrusive andesite (unit Jia) cut the northern sequence in several places (figs. 2 and 3).

Faults separate the stratigraphic succession described above (Triassic monzonite, Fairview Valley Formation, and northern sequence of the Sidewinder Volcanics) from a complex assemblage of younger rocks that also are assigned to the Sidewinder Volcanics (figs. 2 and 3; table 1). Massive to weakly stratified, dacitic to rhyolitic rocks make up most of this assemblage. The relatively coarse grained (crystal-rich) rocks of units Jsdc and Jsdcq (figs. 4H and 6A–B) are ignimbrites that Schermer and Busby (1994) and Schermer and others (2002) assigned to their Middle Jurassic (~163–164 Ma) tuffs of Sidewinder Mountain and Turtle Mountain. An ignimbrite sample from unit Jsdc was dated at 164±2 Ma during this study. An associated fine-grained (crystal-poor) unit (Jsdf) could be either intrusive or extrusive. Also present are laminated rhyolite (unit Jslr) and conglomeratic rocks (unit Jscg). The younger Sidewinder rocks are intruded by undated quartz porphyry (unit Jqp, fig. 6C). All of these rocks, including the quartz porphyry, are intruded by Late Jurassic (153±3 Ma; this report) quartz monzonite porphyry (unit Jqmp, fig. 6D).

Numerous northwest-striking dikes, some of which are dated as Late Jurassic, cut Triassic monzonite, the Fairview Valley Formation, and the Sidewinder Volcanics (figs. 2 and 3). Felsic dikes (unit Jfd) predominate, but dikes of intermediate and mafic composition (units Jid, Jmd) are also present. Schermer and others (2002) dated a felsic dike in the area (fig. 2, loc. AV13) as 152±6 Ma, and a porphyritic dike of intermediate (monzonite to quartz monzonite) composition was dated as 154±2 Ma as part of this study. The dated felsic dike cuts a fault (fig. 2) that separates Triassic monzonite (unit ᵀRm) from the ~153 Ma quartz monzonite porphyry (unit Jqmp). This age relation limits movement on this fault to a brief time interval in the Late Jurassic.

Bedrock outcrops southwest of the Helendale Fault are mostly granitic rocks of Cretaceous and (or) Jurassic age (unit KJg), which we did not examine in detail. In addition, however, Triassic monzonite (unit ᵀRm), crystal-rich dacitic tuff of the Sidewinder Volcanics (unit Jsdc), and a thick felsic dike (unit Jfd) locally crop out adjacent to the fault. The presence of these rocks, particularly the Triassic monzonite (fig. 2), appears to limit right-lateral offset on the Helendale Fault to about 1 km or less (Miller, 1977).

Samples for Geochronologic and Geochemical Analysis

Table 2 lists and describes the twelve samples for which geochronologic and (or) geochemical data are presented in this report, and figure 2 shows the sample localities. Also shown on figure 2 are the localities of sample BM2 of Barth and Wooden (2006) and sample BM15 of Fohey-Breting and others (2010), which are discussed below.

Geochronologic Data

Methods

The uranium-thorium-lead (U-Th-Pb) analyses reported here were carried out on the U.S. Geological Survey (USGS) SHRIMP-RG (Sensitive High Resolution Ion MicroProbe–Reverse Geometry) ion microprobe at Stanford University. Zircons were separated from 2–5 kg samples of sandstone and igneous rocks using standard processing techniques. Individual zircons from mineral separates were mounted in epoxy, polished, and coated with gold prior to analysis. Homogeneous spots in the interiors of detrital zircons were analyzed based on cathodoluminescence (CL) and reflected light photomicrographs, without attempting to sort by grain size or shape. Relatively homogeneous spots within compositionally zoned zircons from igneous rocks were selected based on CL images. A small number of zircon grains in igneous rock samples 846 and 949 yielded statistically younger $^{238}U/^{206}Pb$ ages than the main populations, presumably due to loss of radiogenic Pb, and were excluded from the age calculations.

Igneous Units

Zircons from five igneous units in the Black Mountain area were analyzed. The sampled units are (1) monzonite (sample BM2, unit ℞m), (2) rhyolitic tuff of the northern sequence of the Sidewinder Volcanics (sample BM15, unit Jsnr), (3) coarse-grained (crystal-rich) dacitic tuff of the Sidewinder Volcanics (sample 840, unit Jsdc), (4) a dike of intermediate (monzonite to quartz monzonite) composition (sample 846, unit Jid), and (5) quartz monzonite porphyry (sample 949, unit Jqmp). Analytical data for samples 840, 846, and 949 are presented in table 3 and depicted graphically in figure 7. Data for samples BM2 and BM15 are presented by Barth and Wooden (2006) and Fohey-Breting and others (2010), respectively, and are not included here.

Monzonite (Unit ℞m)

Analysis of 12 zircon grains from sample BM2 yielded a weighted mean age of 244±2 Ma for the Triassic monzonite (Barth and Wooden, 2006). Previous age determinations for this unit using thermal ionization mass spectrometry (TIMS) of bulk zircon fractions ranged from 241±2 to 243±2 Ma (Miller and others, 1995; Barth and others, 1997). The preferred age of 244±2 Ma straddles the currently accepted Early to Middle Triassic boundary of 245.0±1.5 Ma (U.S. Geological Survey Geologic Names Committee, 2010; Walker and Geissman, 2009).

Sidewinder Volcanics, Rhyolite of Northern Sequence (Unit Jsnr)

Analysis of 10 zircon grains from sample BM15 in the rhyolite unit (tuff of Black Mountain of Schermer and others, 2002) yielded individual ages of ~167–184 Ma and a coherent group of 7 grains with a weighted mean age of 181±3 Ma (late Early Jurassic), the interpreted magmatic age of the sample (Fohey-Breting and others, 2010). This age is comparable to a TIMS age of 179.4±3.4 Ma reported by Schermer and others (2002) for rocks they assigned to the tuff of Black Mountain 6 km east of the present study area.

Sidewinder Volcanics, Dacitic to Rhyolitic Rocks, Coarse-grained (Crystal-rich) Facies (Unit Jsdc)

Analysis of eight zircon grains from sample 840 yielded a weighted mean age of 164±2 Ma (late Middle Jurassic). Schermer and others (2002) assigned the sampled rocks to their 164-Ma tuff of Sidewinder Mountain. Our data are consistent with this correlation but also would be consistent with correlation to the lithologically similar 163-Ma tuff of Turtle Mountain of Schermer and others (2002). We infer the sampled rocks to be juxtaposed against the Fairview Valley Formation by a fault that is intruded by a felsic dike (unit Jfd; fig. 2), an interpretation previously suggested by Miller (1977).

Intermediate-composition Dike (Unit Jid)

Analysis of 10 zircon grains from sample 846 yielded a coherent group of 9 grains with a weighted mean age of 154±2 Ma (Late Jurassic). The age calculation excluded the youngest analyzed grain, which is presumed to have undergone Pb loss. The sampled dike is cut by a felsic dike (unit Jfd) a short distance south of the sample locality (fig. 2), consistent with the ~152 Ma age reported for another felsic dike in the study area by Schermer and others (2002).

Quartz Monzonite Porphyry (Unit Jqmp)

Analysis of 14 zircon grains from sample 949 yielded a coherent group of 11 grains with a weighted mean age of 153±3 Ma (Late Jurassic). The age calculation excluded the three youngest analyzed grains, which are presumed to have undergone Pb loss. Because the ~153 Ma age of this sample is within analytical error of the ~154 Ma age of sample 846, it is possible that the quartz monzonite porphyry (unit Jqmp) and the intermediate-composition dikes (unit Jid), which are lithologically similar, were emplaced during the same intrusive event. The zircon analysis also shows that the quartz monzonite porphyry may be only slightly older than the ~152 Ma felsic dike that cuts it (fig. 2), although the dike could be as young as 146 Ma based on the reported analytical error of ±6 Ma (Schermer and others, 2002).

Sedimentary Units

We analyzed detrital zircons from one arkosic sandstone sample (178) in unit 2 of the Fairview Valley Formation (Jfv$_2$), two arkosic sandstone samples (129 and 159) in unit 3 (Jfv$_3$), and one sample (215) in the overlying quartz-rich sandstone unit (Jqs). We measured the ages of 24–50 randomly selected grains from each sample, sufficient to broadly characterize the age distribution, but not sufficient to ensure that all minor age populations were identified. Analytical data are presented in table 4 and depicted graphically in figure 8.

Fairview Valley Formation

We analyzed 50 detrital zircon grains from sample 129, 24 from sample 159, and 30 from sample 178. All three samples are dominated by Paleoproterozoic grains with ages between about 1640 and 1750 Ma (75 percent in sample 129; 56 percent in sample 159; 60 percent in sample 178). The remaining grains are mostly Mesoproterozoic to latest Paleoproterozoic in age (~1022–1632 Ma). In addition, however, sample 178 contains one Permian grain, one Triassic grain, and most significantly, 7 grains (23 percent) of Early Jurassic age (~191–198 Ma). These 7 grains constitute a statistically significant population (coherent group) that yields a weighted mean age of 194±2 Ma. We consider this to be a reasonable estimate of the maximum depositional age of unit 2 of the Fairview Valley Formation, assuming that all 7 grains represent a single igneous source rock.

Quartz-rich Sandstone Unit (Jqs)

We analyzed 25 detrital zircon grains from sample 215. This analysis yielded a heterogeneous distribution of ages, including Archean (2 grains), Paleoproterozoic (5 grains), Mesoproterozoic (9 grains), Neoproterozoic (5 grains), Paleozoic (2 grains), and Jurassic (2 grains). These ages do not precisely limit the maximum depositional age of the sandstone unit, but the two Jurassic ages of 172±2 and 185±4 Ma are within the range of ages reported by Fohey-Breting and others (2010) for individual zircons from the overlying rhyolite of the Sidewinder Volcanics (sample BM15). Thus, it is likely that the sandstone unit is not significantly older than the rhyolite.

Provenance

The predominance of Paleoproterozoic zircons in the samples from the Fairview Valley Formation is consistent with derivation of detritus from local crystalline basement rocks (Wooden and Miller, 1990; Barth and others, 2009). By contrast, the more heterogeneous distribution of ages in the overlying quartzose sandstone unit is similar to that reported by Dickinson and Gehrels (2003) from Jurassic eolian sandstones of the Colorado Plateau, which they interpreted to be derived from various distant sources including the Appalachian orogen.

The Early Jurassic (~191–198 Ma) zircons in Fairview Valley Formation sample 178 are of unknown provenance. Because plutons of this age have not been identified in the Mojave Desert region, these zircons may have been derived from local volcanic sources that are either not preserved or not yet dated. Detrital zircons of similar age also have been reported in the Jurassic(?) and Cretaceous McCoy Mountains Formation about 250 km southeast of Black Mountain (Barth and others, 2004; Spencer and others, 2011).

Geochemical Data

Whole-rock X-ray fluorescence (XRF) analyses of seven samples of igneous rocks from the Black Mountain area were performed in December 2006 at Michigan State University using a Bruker S4 Pioneer spectrometer. These analyses provide a general idea of the composition of selected map units for comparison with rocks of the Sidewinder Volcanics previously analyzed by Fohey-Breting and others (2010). Data from our analyses are presented in table 5, and selected data are plotted graphically (fig. 9) on a total alkali–silica (TAS) diagram (Best and Christiansen, 2001; LeMaitre and others, 2002) and the cation plot of Jensen (1976).

Four samples are from Middle Jurassic dacitic to rhyolitic rocks of the Sidewinder Volcanics. Two of these samples (840, 1072) are from the coarse-grained facies (unit Jsdc) and one sample (1435) is from the coarse-grained facies with abundant quartz (unit Jsdcq). These three samples plot on or just above the trachydacite-dacite boundary on the TAS diagram and on or near the tholeiitic rhyolite to calc-alkaline dacite boundary on the Jensen plot (fig. 9). By contrast, sample 1104 from the fine-grained facies (unit Jsdf) is of rhyolitic composition. The other three samples are from fine-grained to porphyritic intrusive units that are closely associated with Sidewinder volcanic rocks. On the TAS diagram these samples range in composition from andesite (sample 1250, unit Jia) to borderline dacite/rhyolite/trachydacite (sample 949, unit Jqmp) to rhyolite (sample 935, unit Jqp), or their plutonic equivalents (fig. 9).

Also shown on both the TAS and Jensen plots (fig. 9) are samples of the tuffs of Black Mountain and Turtle Mountain that were analyzed by Fohey-Breting and others (2010). These analyses confirm the dominantly rhyolitic composition of the tuff of Black Mountain (equivalent to our unit Jsnr) in contrast to the dacitic composition of the younger tuff of Turtle Mountain. Our samples 840, 1072, and 1435 compare closely with samples analyzed by Fohey-Breting and others (2010) from the tuff of Turtle Mountain, but are slightly more alkaline.

Paleozoic to Jurassic History

During the Paleozoic the Black Mountain area was part of the western North American continental shelf, where carbonate strata accumulated in shallow marine water (Miller, 1977, 1981). In late Early or early Middle Triassic time (~244 Ma), the Paleozoic rocks were intruded by a monzonite pluton that was part of the nascent Mesozoic magmatic arc of western North America (Barth and others, 1997; Barth and Wooden, 2006). The Triassic arc is thought to have developed after truncation of the Paleozoic miogeocline along a northwest-striking, sinistral fault zone at the edge of the continent (Stevens and others, 2005). Deformation and metamorphism of the Paleozoic strata preceded magmatism (Miller, 1977, 1981).

Exhumation of the Triassic monzonite was followed by Early Jurassic deposition of the Fairview Valley Formation. Detrital zircons from the Fairview Valley Formation indicate that deposition began no earlier than about 194 Ma. The abundance of conglomerate and the lack of *in situ* marine fossils suggest a nonmarine or marginal marine depositional setting (Miller, 1978; Schermer and others, 2002). Arkosic sandstone in the lower and middle parts of the formation was derived from local Proterozoic crystalline rocks and subordinate Early Jurassic volcanic rocks. Massive conglomerate in the upper 500 m of the formation probably represents alluvial-fan deposits close to an uplifted source area of Paleozoic limestone.

After deposition, the Fairview Valley Formation was tilted eastward, eroded, and unconformably overlapped by a thin sedimentary sequence that includes conglomerate and quartz-rich sandstone. The presence of conglomerate suggests a nonmarine depositional environment. The provenance of the quartz-rich sandstone was distinct from that of arkosic sandstone in the underlying Fairview Valley Formation, but comparable to that of contemporaneous eolian sand sheets represented by the Navajo Sandstone on the Colorado Plateau (Schermer and others, 2002).

Deposition of the quartz-rich sandstone was closely followed by the extrusion of rhyolitic ignimbrite that constitutes the oldest part of the Jurassic Sidewinder Volcanics (tuff of Black Mountain) at about 181 Ma. Voluminous late Middle Jurassic (~163–164 Ma) dacitic ignimbrites (equivalent to the tuffs of Sidewinder and/or Turtle Mountain) were extruded later, although the stratigraphic relations between these ignimbrites and the tuff of Black Mountain are obscured by faulting. Late Jurassic magmatic activity in the area included the intrusion of northwest-striking dikes of felsic to mafic composition and a pluton of quartz monzonite porphyry between about 152 and 154 Ma.

Regionally, the Sidewinder Volcanics are interpreted as a nested caldera complex that includes four successive, widespread ignimbrites ranging in age from ~181 to ~151 Ma (Schermer and Busby, 1994; Schermer and others, 2002; Fohey-Breting and others, 2010). The Sidewinder Volcanics and the associated Jurassic intrusive rocks formed as part of a northwest-trending Andean arc that extended the length of the western North American continental margin (Tosdal and others, 1989; Saleeby and Busby-Spera, 1992; Barth and others, 2008).

Middle(?) and Late Jurassic deformation of rocks in the Black Mountain area included northward tilting, faulting, and folding. Many details of the structural chronology remain unclear, and conflicting interpretations have been proposed (Miller, 1977; Schermer, 1993; Schermer and others, 2002). Most of the deformation, however, likely predated intrusion of the Late Jurassic dikes, although Schermer (1993) and Schermer and others (2002) interpreted the folding to be younger. Some faulting postdated intrusion of ~153 Ma quartz monzonite porphyry and predated intrusion of the ~152 Ma felsic dike dated by Schermer and others (2002), and other faulting could be even younger.

Summary

U-Pb geochronologic data presented here and elsewhere (Barth and Wooden, 2006; Fohey-Breting and others, 2010) provide an updated chronology of Mesozoic magmatic and depositional events in the Black Mountain area (fig. 10): (1) intrusion of a late Early to early Middle Triassic (~244 Ma) monzonite pluton; (2) Early Jurassic (no earlier than ~194 Ma) deposition of the Fairview Valley Formation, a thick sequence of mudstone, siltstone, sandstone, and conglomerate; (3) late Early Jurassic deposition of a thin sedimentary sequence, primarily conglomerate and sandstone, followed closely by extrusion of a thick rhyolitic ignimbrite (tuff of Black Mountain) at about 181 Ma; (4) late Middle Jurassic (~164 Ma) extrusion of crystal-rich, dacitic ignimbrite (tuff of Sidewinder Mountain or tuff of Turtle Mountain); and (5) Late Jurassic intrusion of intermediate-composition dikes (~154 Ma) and quartz monzonite porphyry (~153

Ma). Intrusion of younger (152±6 Ma) felsic dikes (Schermer and others, 2002) followed faulting that postdated intrusion of the ~153 Ma quartz monzonite porphyry. The geochronologic data presented in this report, together with new geochemical data for selected rock units, supplement the geologic map of Stone (2006) and help clarify the tectonic evolution of the western Mojave Desert region.

Acknowledgments

We extend our appreciation to the staff of CEMEX for granting access to Black Mountain Quarry and the adjacent company-owned lands. The logistical assistance of Gerry Frankovich, quarry manager in May 2006, was especially helpful. Cal Stevens (San Jose State University) visited the map area and contributed to some of the stratigraphic and structural interpretations. Discussions with Brett Cox and David Miller (U.S. Geological Survey) led to significant improvements in the final manuscript. Geochronologic work was in part supported by the National Science Foundation through grants EAR-0408730 and EAR-0711119.

References Cited

Aksoy, R., 1993, The Helendale Fault Zone: Progress in Earthquake Research and Engineering, v. 4, p. 17–29.

Barth, A.P., Tosdal, R.M., Wooden, J.L., and Howard, K.A., 1997, Triassic plutonism in southern California—Southward younging of arc initiation along a truncated continental margin: Tectonics, v. 16, no. 2, p. 290–304.

Barth, A.P., and Wooden, J.L., 2006, Timing of magmatism following initial convergence at a passive margin, southwestern U.S. Cordillera, and ages of lower crustal magma sources: Journal of Geology, v. 114, p. 231–245.

Barth, A.P., Wooden, J.L., Coleman, D.S., and Vogel, M.B., 2009, Assembling and disassembling California—A zircon and monazite geochronologic framework for Proterozoic crustal evolution in southern California: Journal of Geology, v. 117, p. 221–239.

Barth, A.P., Wooden, J.L., Howard, K.A., and Richards, J.L., 2008, Late Jurassic plutonism in the southwest U.S. Cordillera, in Wright, J.E., and Shervais, J.W. (eds.), Arcs, ophiolites, and batholiths—A tribute to Cliff Hopson: Geological Society of America Special Paper 438, p. 379–406.

Barth, A.P., Wooden, J.L., Jacobson, C.E., and Probst, Kelly, 2004, U-Pb geochronology and geochemistry of the McCoy Mountains Formation, southeastern California—A Cretaceous retroarc foreland basin: Geological Society of America Bulletin, v. 116, p. 142–153.

Best, M.G., and Christiansen, E.H., 2001, Igneous petrology: Malden, Mass., Blackwell Science, 458 p.

Bowen, O.E., Jr., 1954, Geology and mineral deposits of Barstow quadrangle, San Bernardino County, California: California Division of Mines Bulletin 165, p. 5–185, scale 1:125,000.

Dibblee, T.W., Jr., 1960, Preliminary geologic map of the Apple Valley quadrangle, California: U.S. Geological Survey Mineral Investigations Field Studies Map MF-232, scale 1:62,500.

Dibblee, T.W., Jr., 1967, Areal geology of the western Mojave Desert, California: U.S. Geological Survey Professional Paper 522, 153 p., scale 1:125,000.

Dickinson, W.R., and Gehrels, G.E., 2003, U-Pb ages of detrital zircons from Permian and Jurassic eolian sandstones of the Colorado Plateau, USA—Paleogeographic implications: Sedimentary Geology, v. 163, p. 29–66.

Dokka, R.K., and Travis, C.J., 1990, Late Cenozoic strike-slip faulting in the Mojave Desert, California: Tectonics, v. 9, p. 311–340.

Fohey-Breting, N.K., Barth, A.P., Wooden, J.L., Mazdab, F.K., Carter, C.A., and Schermer, E.R., 2010, Relationship of voluminous ignimbrites to continental arc plutons—Petrology of Jurassic ignimbrites and contemporaneous plutons in southern California: Journal of Volcanology and Geothermal Research, v. 189, p. 1–11.

Jensen, L.S., 1976, A new cation plot for classifying subalkalic volcanic rocks: Ontario Division of Mines, Miscellaneous Paper 66, 22 p.

LeMaitre, R.W. and 14 others, 2002, Igneous rocks, a classification and glossary of terms: Cambridge, U.K., Press Syndicate of the University of Cambridge, 236 p.

Miller, E.L., 1977, Geology of the Victorville region, California: Houston, Tex., Rice University, Ph.D. dissertation, 226 p.

Miller, E.L., 1978, The Fairview Valley Formation—A Mesozoic intraorogenic deposit in the southwestern Mojave Desert, in Howell, D.G., and McDougall, K.A., eds., Mesozoic paleogeography of the western United States: Society of Economic Paleontologists and Mineralogists, Pacific Section, book 8, p. 277–282.

Miller, E.L., 1981, Geology of the Victorville region, California: Geological Society of America Bulletin, pt. 2, v. 92, p. 554–608.

Miller, F.K., and Morton, D.M., 1980, Potassium-argon geochronology of the eastern Transverse Ranges and southern Mojave Desert, southern California: U.S. Geological Survey Professional Paper 1152, 30 p.

Miller, J.S., Glazner, A.F., Walker, J.D., and Martin, M.W., 1995, Geochronologic and isotopic evidence for Triassic-Jurassic emplacement of the eugeoclinal allochthon in the Mojave Desert region, California: Geological Society of America Bulletin, v. 107, p. 1441–1457.

Petersen, M.D., and Wesnousky, S.G., 1994, Fault slip rates and earthquake histories for active faults in southern California: Bulletin of the Seismological Society of America, v. 84, no. 5, p. 1608–1649.

Saleeby, J.B., and Busby-Spera, Cathy, 1992, Early Mesozoic tectonic evolution of the western U.S. Cordillera, in Burchfiel, B.C., Lipman, P.W., and Zoback, M.L., eds., The Cordilleran orogen—Conterminous U.S.: Boulder, Col., Geological Society of America, The Geology of North America, v. G-3, p. 107–168.

Sauber, Jeanne, Thatcher, Wayne, Solomon, S.C., and Lisowski, Michael, 1994, Geodetic slip rate for the Eastern California shear zone and the recurrence time of Mojave Desert earthquakes: Nature, v. 367, no. 6460, p. 264–266.

Schermer, E.R., 1993, Mesozoic structural evolution of the west-central Mojave Desert, in Howell, D.G., and McDougall, K.A., eds., Mesozoic paleogeography of the western United States: Society of Economic Paleontologists and Mineralogists, Pacific Section, book 8, p. 307–321.

Schermer, E.R., and Busby, Cathy, 1994, Jurassic magmatism in the central Mojave Desert— Implications for arc paleogeography and preservation of continental volcanic sequences: Geological Society of America Bulletin, v. 106, p. 767–790.

Schermer, E.R., Busby, C.J., and Mattinson, J.M., 2002, Paleogeographic and tectonic implications of Jurassic sedimentary and volcanic sequences in the central Mojave block, in Glazner, A.F., Walker, J.D., and Bartley, J.M., eds., Geologic evolution of the Mojave Desert and southwestern Basin and Range: Geological Society of America Memoir 195, p. 93–115.

Spencer, J.E., Richard, S.M., Gehrels, G.E., Gleason, J.D., and Dickinson, W.R., 2011, Age and tectonic setting of the Mesozoic McCoy Mountains Formation in western Arizona, USA: Geological Society of America Bulletin, v. 123, p. 1258–1274.

Stevens, C.H., Stone, Paul, and Miller, J.S., 2005, A new reconstruction of the Paleozoic continental margin of southwestern North America—Implications for the nature and timing of continental truncation and the possible role of the Mojave-Sonora megashear, *in* Anderson, T.H., Nourse, J.A., McKee, J.W., and Steiner, M.B., eds., The Mojave-Sonora megashear hypothesis—Development, assessment, and alternatives: Geological Society of America Special Paper 393, p. 597–618.

Stone, Paul, 2006, Preliminary geologic map of the Black Mountain area northeast of Victorville, San Bernardino County, California: U.S. Geological Survey Open-File Report 2006-1347, scale 1:12,000.

Stone, Paul, Barth, A.P., and Wooden, J.L., 2005, U-Pb detrital zircon data from metasedimentary rocks at Black Mountain near Victorville, California—Implications for the age of the early Mesozoic Fairview Valley Formation [abs.]: Geological Society of America Abstracts with Programs, v. 37, no. 4, p. 86.

Stone, W.D., 1964, Geology of the Black Mountain area, Apple Valley quadrangle, California: Riverside, University of California, master's thesis, 127 p.

Tosdal, R.M., Haxel, G.B., and Wright, J.E., 1989, Jurassic geology of the Sonoran Desert region, southern Arizona, southeastern California, and northernmost Sonora—Construction of a continental-margin magmatic arc, *in* Jenney, J.P., and Reynolds, S.J., Geologic evolution of Arizona: Arizona Geological Society Digest 17, p. 397–434.

U.S. Geological Survey Geologic Names Committee, 2010, Divisions of geologic time—Major chronostratigraphic and geochronologic units: U.S. Geological Survey Fact Sheet 2010–3059, 2 p.

Walker, J.D., 1985, Permo-Triassic paleogeography and tectonics of the southwestern United States: Cambridge, Massachusetts Institute of Technology, Ph. D. dissertation, 224 p.

Walker, J.D., 1987, Permian to Middle Triassic rocks of the Mojave Desert, *in* Dickinson, W.R., and Klute, M.A., eds., Mesozoic rocks of southern Arizona and adjacent areas: Arizona Geological Society Digest, v. 18, p. 1–14.

Walker, J.D., and Geissman, J.W., compilers, 2009, Geologic time scale: Geological Society of America, doi: 10.1130/2009.CTS004R2C.

Wooden, J.L., and Miller, D.M., 1990, Chronologic and isotopic framework for Early Proterozoic crustal evolution in the eastern Mojave Desert region, SE California: Journal of Geophysical Research, v. 95, no. B12, p. 20,133–20,146.

Figures 1–10 and Tables 1–5 follow.

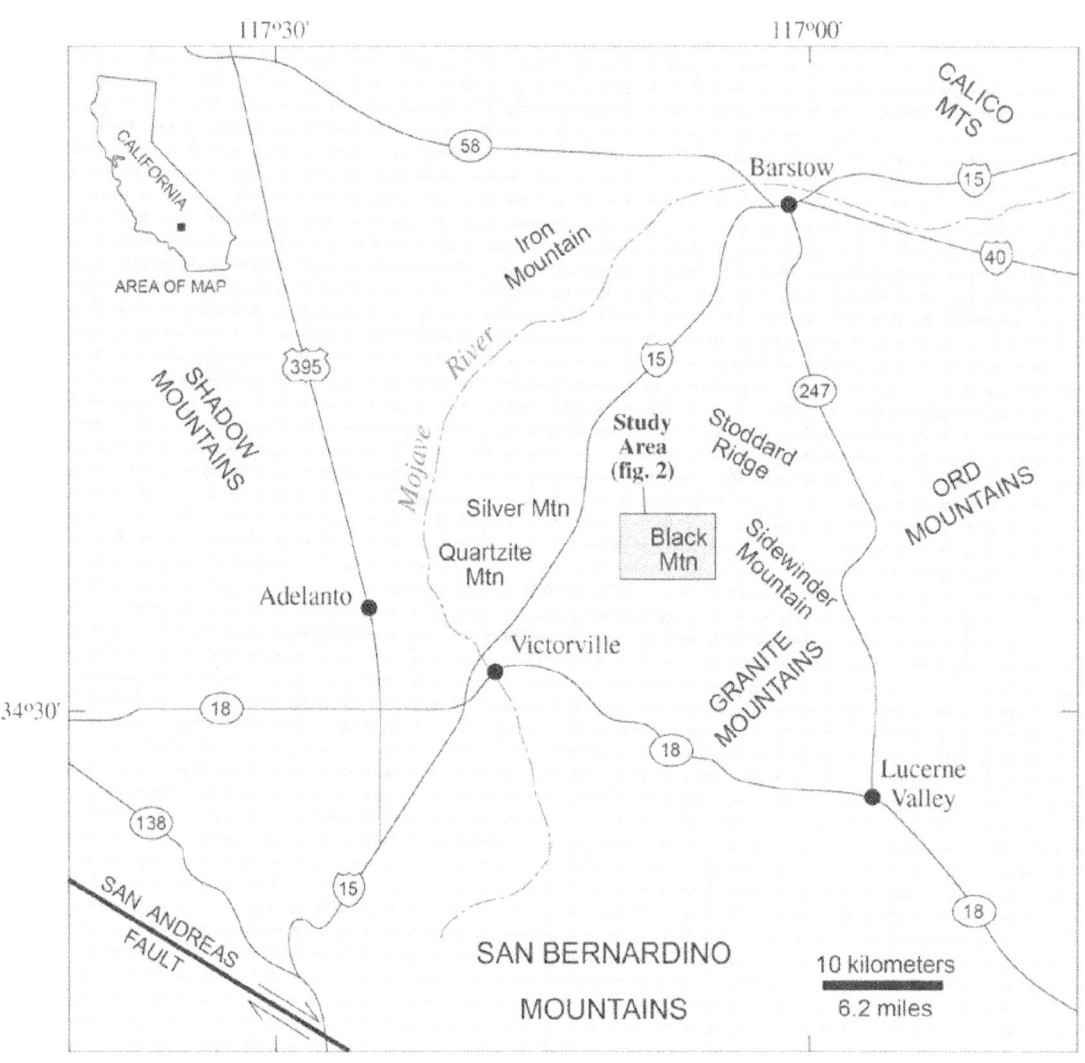

Figure 1. Map showing location of Black Mountain area northeast of Victorville in San Bernardino County, California.

Figure 2. Geologic map of Black Mountain area (see figure 1 for location of area). Reduced and modified from Stone (2006).

13

ml	Modified land
mw	Mine waste
q	Quarry
Qya	Young alluvium (Quaternary)
Qc	Colluvium and talus (Quaternary)
Qia	Intermediate-age alluvium (Quaternary)
QToa	Old alluvium (Quaternary and/or Tertiary)
KJg	Granite (Cretaceous and/or Jurassic)
KJps	Plutonic rocks near Sidewinder Mine (Cretaceous and/or Jurassic)
KJmp	Monzonite porphyry (Cretaceous or Jurassic)

Dikes (Late Jurassic)

Jfd	Felsic dikes
Jid	Intermediate-composition dikes
Jmd	Mafic dikes
Jqmp	Quartz monzonite porphyry (Late Jurassic)
Jqp	Quartz porphyry (Late or Middle Jurassic?)
Jia	Intrusive andesite (Late or Middle Jurassic?)

Sidewinder Volcanics (Jurassic)

Dacitic to rhyolitic rocks (Middle Jurassic)

Jsd	Undivided
Jsdf	Fine-grained (crystal-poor) facies
Jsdc	Coarse-grained (crystal-rich) facies
Jsdcq	Quartz-rich coarse-grained facies
Jslr	Laminated rhyolite (Middle Jurassic?)
Jscg	Conglomeratic rocks (Middle Jurassic?)

Northern sequence (Early Jurassic)

Jsnr	Rhyolite
Jsnl	Laminated volcanic rocks
Jsnq	Quartzose sandstone
Jsns	Sandstone and conglomerate

Unnamed sedimentary rocks (Early Jurassic)

Jqs	Quartz-rich sandstone
Jch	Calc-hornfels
Jslc	Sandy limestone conglomerate
Jvc	Volcanic conglomerate

Fairview Valley Formation (Early Jurassic)

Jfv$_5$	Unit 5
Jfv$_4$	Unit 4
Jfv$_3$	Unit 3
Jfv$_2$	Unit 2
Jfv$_1$	Unit 1
Tim	Monzonite (Middle or Early Triassic)
M$_z$P$_z$m	Siliceous marble (Mesozoic or Paleozoic)
M$_z$P$_z$q	Quartzite (Mesozoic or Paleozoic)
P$_z$mc	Marble and calc-silicate rocks (Paleozoic)
P$_z$m	Marble (Paleozoic)

————	Contact — Dotted where concealed
⇌	Fault — Arrows show sense of lateral displacement. Dashed where approximately located, dotted where concealed or intruded, queried where uncertain
————	Conglomerate bed in unit 3 of Fairview Valley Formation
——⊦——	Syncline—Showing direction of plunge
——⋈——	Antiform in overturned beds—Showing direction of plunge
60	Strike and dip of beds, inclined
60	Strike and dip of beds, overturned
●	Sample locality (this report)
✱	Sample locality (Schermer and others, 2002)
■	Sample locality (Barth and Wooden, 2006)
▲	Sample locality (Fohey-Breting and others, 2010)

Figure 2 (explanation).

14

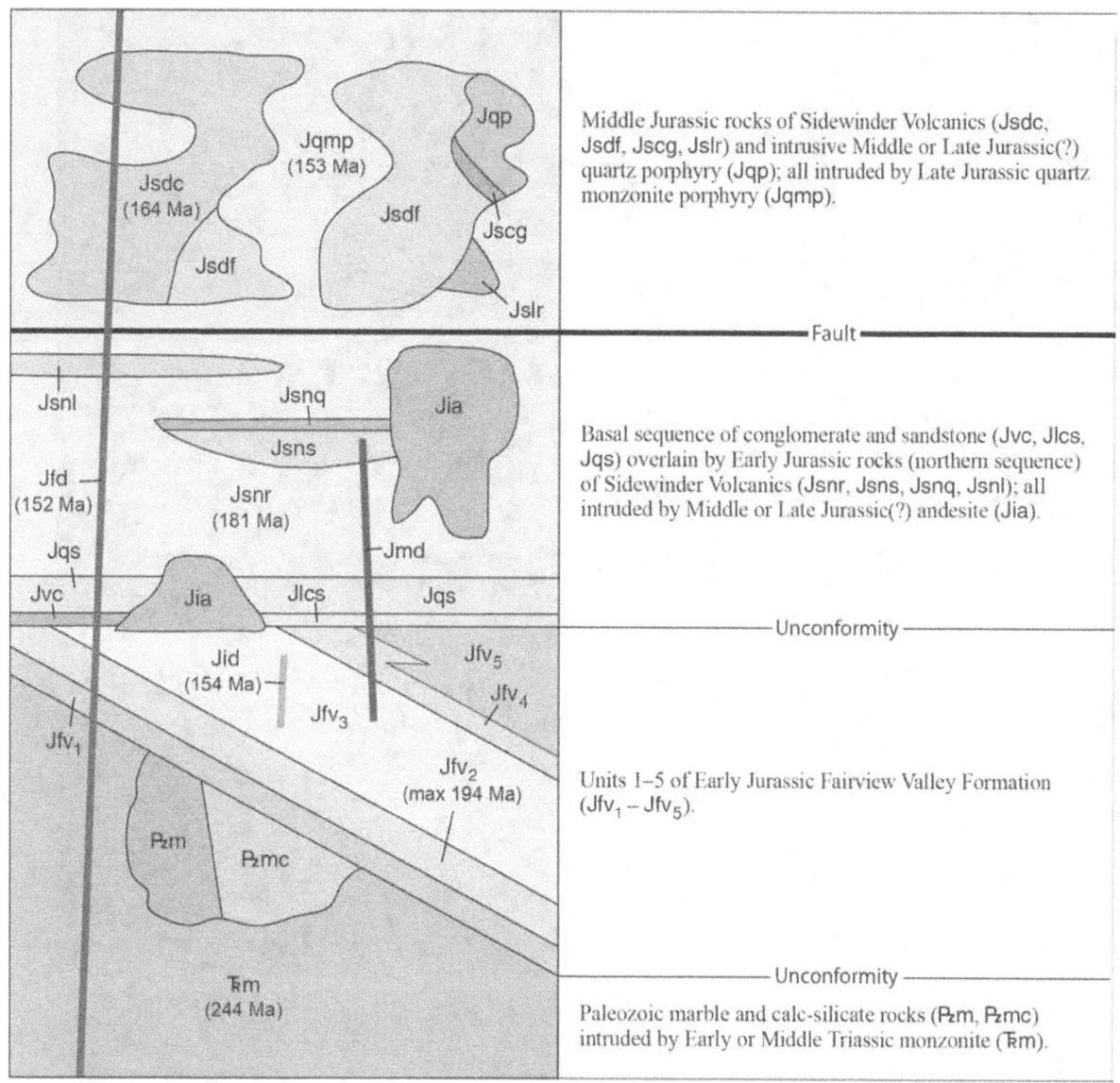

Figure 3. Schematic diagram illustrating stratigraphic relations of Jurassic and older rocks in the Black Mountain area. Unit symbols and colors as in figure 2. Approximate numerical ages, based on U-Pb geochronology, are shown in parentheses.

15

Figure 4. Photographs showing characteristic outcrops of selected rock units, Black Mountain area. *A,* Paleozoic marble and calc-silicate rocks (unit Pzmc); *B,* basal conglomerate composed of plutonic clasts, Fairview Valley Formation, unit 1 (Jfv$_1$); *C,* banded mudstone and siltstone, Fairview Valley Formation, unit 2 (Jfv$_2$); *D,* calcareous siltstone, Fairview Valley Formation, unit 3 (Jfv$_3$); *E,* conglomerate containing white marble clasts, Fairview Valley Formation, unit 3 (Jfv$_3$); *F,* limestone conglomerate, Fairview Valley Formation, unit 5 (Jfv$_5$); *G,* crystal-poor rhyolitic tuff with flattened clasts, Sidewinder Volcanics (unit Jsnr); *H,* crystal-rich dacitic tuff with flattened clasts, Sidewinder Volcanics (unit Jsdcq).

Figure 5. Photographs showing folds in unit 3 (Jfv₃) of Fairview Valley Formation. *A*, isolated outcrop-scale synformal fold in middle part of unit, view to the southeast; and *B*, hinge of map-scale syncline in uppermost part of unit, directly below contact with unit 4, view to the northwest.

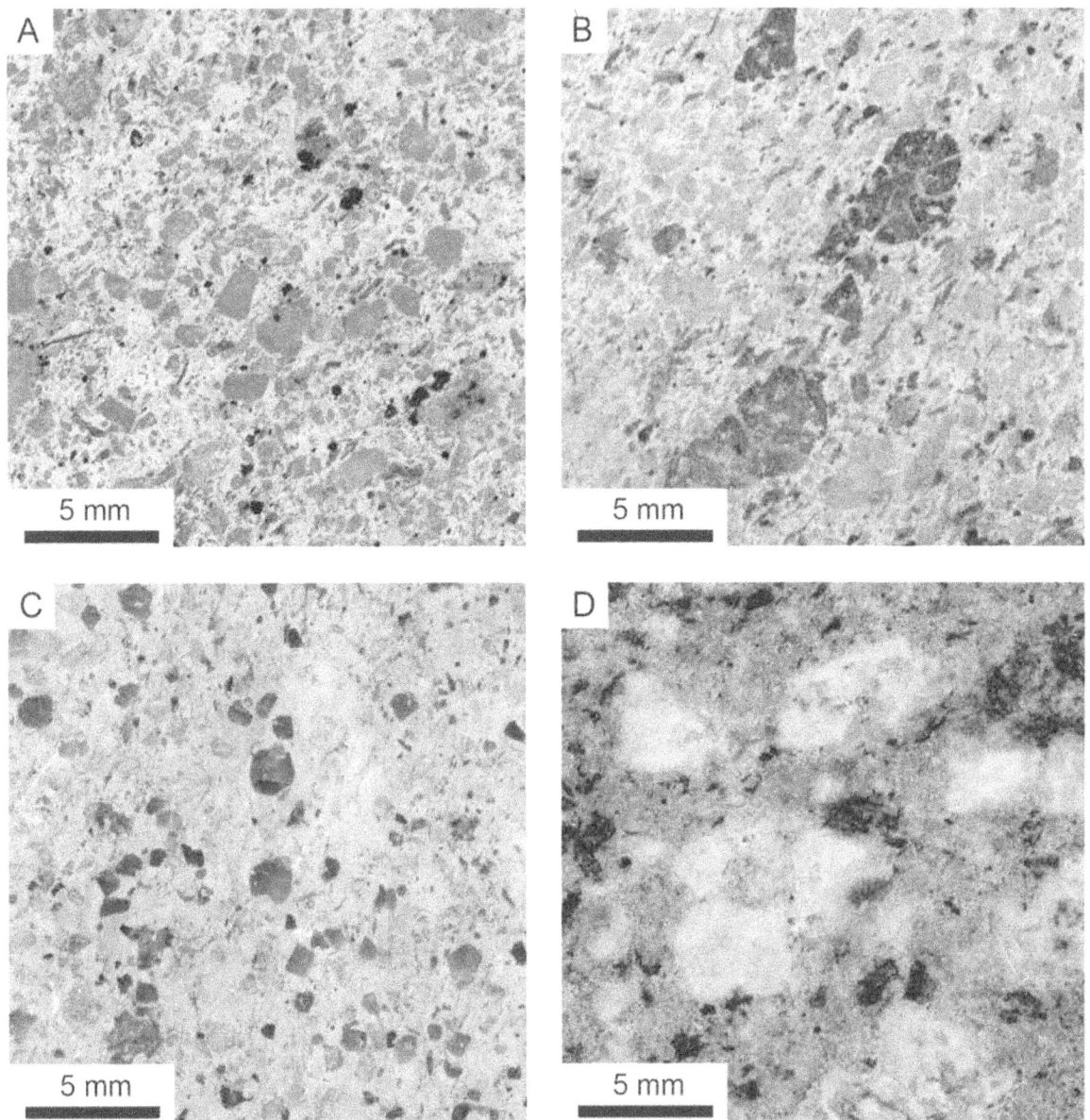

Figure 6. Photographs of stained slabs from selected igneous rock units, Black Mountain area. Potassium feldspar was stained yellow using sodium cobaltinitrite; plagioclase was stained red using amaranth. Quartz is unstained. *A*, crystal-rich dacitic tuff, Sidewinder Volcanics (unit **Jsdc**). Angular plagioclase phenocrysts (stained red) and other grains in a felsic groundmass. *B*, crystal-rich dacitic tuff with abundant quartz, Sidewinder Volcanics (unit **Jsdcq**). Large, embayed quartz phenocrysts (dark gray) and angular plagioclase phenocrysts (stained red) in a felsic groundmass. Angular texture of plagioclase crystals in A and B is ascribed to fragmentation during explosive venting of magma. *C*, quartz porphyry (unit **Jqp**). Quartz phenocrysts (gray) in a felsic groundmass. *D*, quartz monzonite porphyry (unit **Jqmp**). Plagioclase phenocrysts (stained red) and clots of mafic minerals (black) in a felsic groundmass.

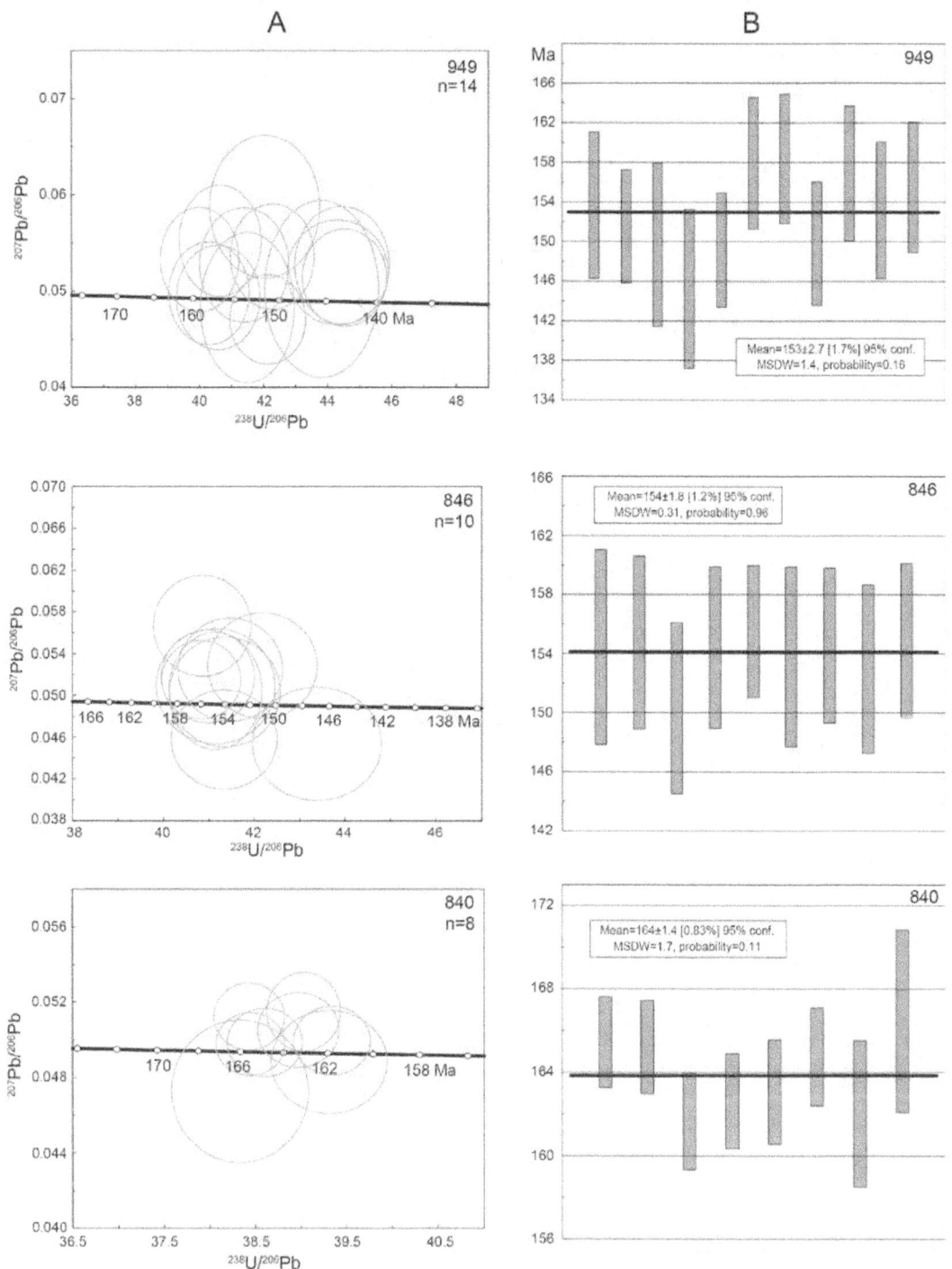

Figure 7. Plots of U-Pb ages of individual zircon grains from selected igneous rocks in the Black Mountain area (sample 840, Sidewinder Volcanics, crystal-rich dacitic tuff, unit Jsdc; sample 846, intermediate-composition dike, unit Jid; sample 949, quartz monzonite porphyry, unit Jqmp). *A*, Tera-Wasserburg concordia plots. *B*, bar diagrams of $^{206}Pb*/^{238}U$ ages with 2-sigma errors; boxes show weighted mean crystallization ages. Note that the youngest grain in sample 846 and the youngest three grains in sample 949 (table 3) were excluded from the calculations of weighted mean age; we infer these grains to have undergone minor Pb loss.

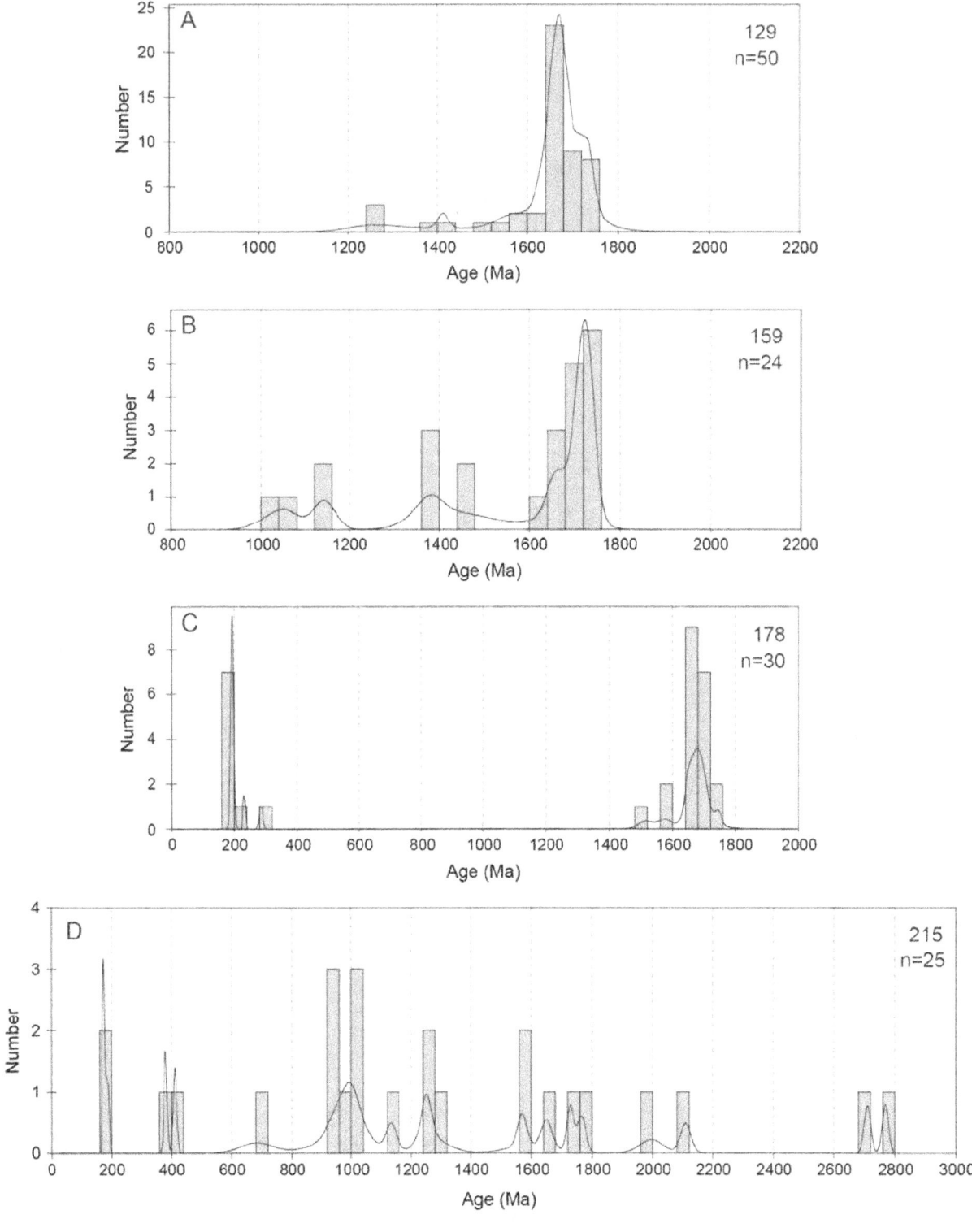

Figure 8. Histograms and cumulative probability curves of U-Pb detrital zircon ages from sandstone samples in the Black Mountain area. A–C, Fairview Valley Formation. *A*, sample 129, and *B*, sample 159, both from unit 3 (Jfv₃); *C*, sample 178, from unit 2 (Jfv₂); *D*, sample 215, quartz-rich sandstone unit (Jqs) above Fairview Valley Formation.

20

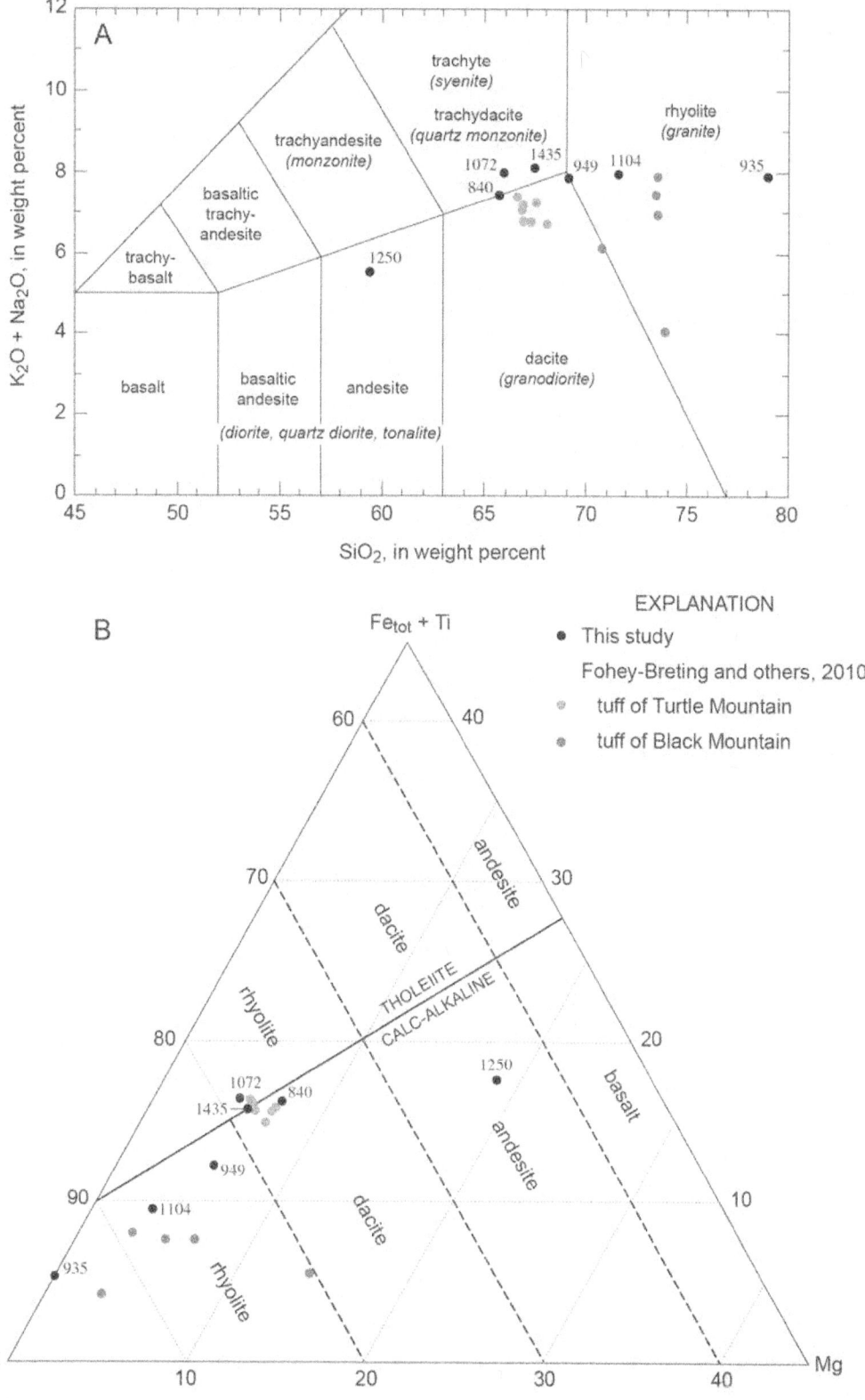

Figure 9. Diagram showing chemical characteristics of igneous rocks analyzed in this study and by Fohey-Breting and others (2010). *A*, total alkali-silica (TAS) plot (Best and Christiansen, 2001; LeMaitre and others, 2002). *B*, Jensen cation plot (Jensen, 1976). Analytical data normalized to 100 percent (volatile-free) with all Fe as FeO.

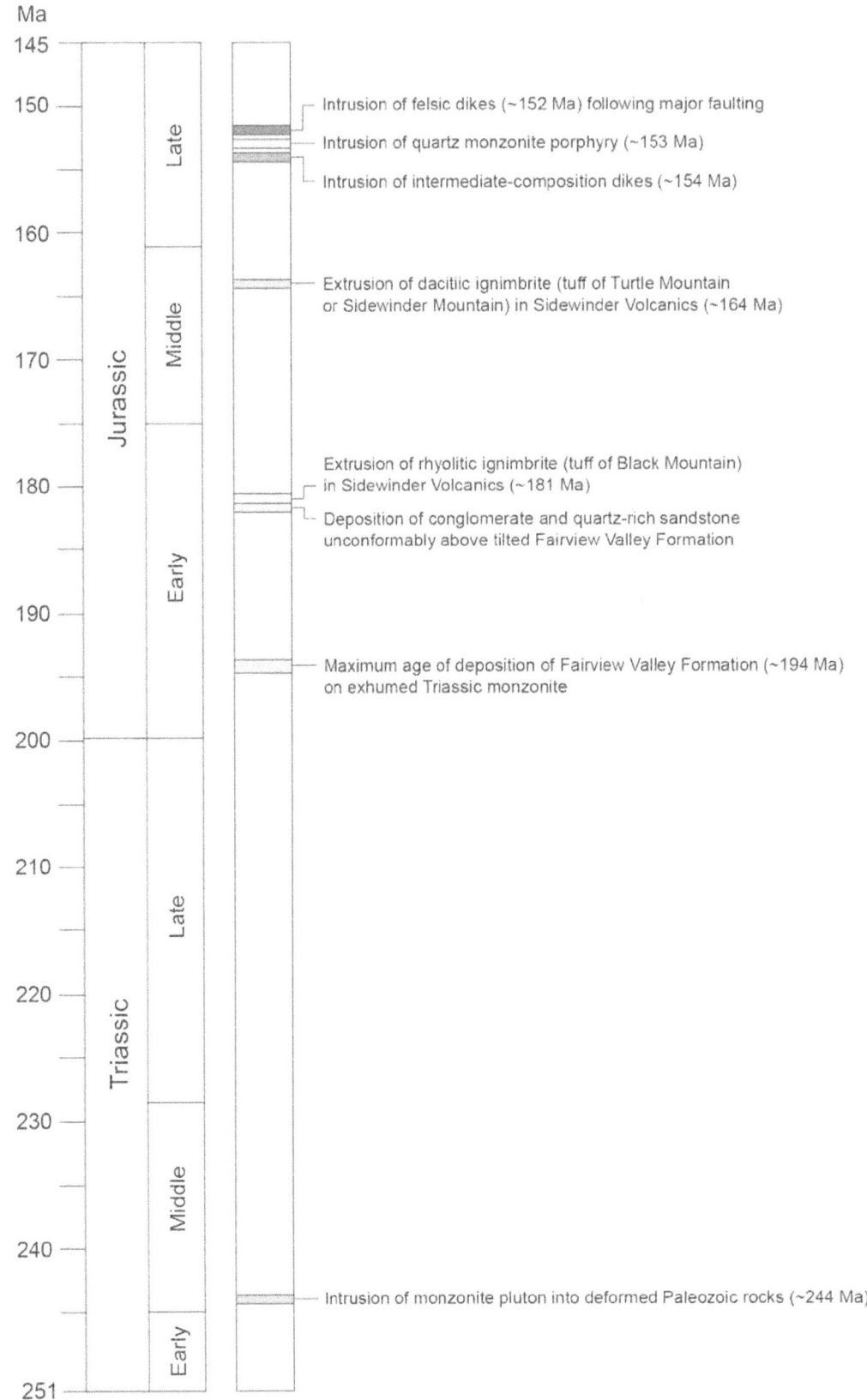

Figure 10. Diagram showing chronology of Triassic and Jurassic magmatic and depositional events in the Black Mountain area. Note that ages of events are approximate and are depicted without error bars for simplicity. Time scale from U.S. Geological Survey Geologic Names Committee (2010).

Table 1. Lithologic descriptions of pre-Cenozoic map units in Black Mountain area, San Bernardino County, California (fig. 2). Modified from Stone (2006).

Symbol	Unit	Lithology	Age
KJg	Granite	Medium- to coarse-grained, light-colored granitic rocks	Cretaceous and/or Jurassic
KJps	Plutonic rocks near Sidewinder Mine	Medium- to coarse-grained granitic rocks, fine- to medium-grained quartz porphyry, and porphyritic dikes of intermediate composition	Cretaceous and/or Jurassic
KJmp	Monzonite porphyry	Granitoid rocks containing 50 percent potassium feldspar and plagioclase phenocrysts ≤10 mm across in a fine-grained groundmass	Cretaceous or Jurassic
	Dikes	Northwest-striking d kes of felsic, intermediate, and mafic composition	Late Jurassic
Jfd	Felsic dikes	Very fine grained felsite dikes	
Jid	Intermediate-composition dikes	Porphyritic monzonite to quartz monzonite d kes	
Jmd	Mafic dikes	Diorite to quartz diorite dikes	
Jqmp	Quartz monzonite porphyry	Granitoid rocks containing 30–50 percent plagioclase, potassium feldspar, and quartz phenocrysts in a fine-grained groundmass. Feldspar phenocrysts ≤10 mm across, quartz phenocrysts ≤3 mm across	Late Jurassic
Jqp	Quartz porphyry	Very fine grained to microcrystalline felsic rocks containing 10–40 percent anhedral to subhedral phenocrysts of quartz ≤3 mm across	Late Jurassic(?)
Jia	Intrusive andesite	Massive, dark, very fine grained rocks composed primarily of plagioclase, mafic minerals, and minor quartz; scattered plagioclase phenocrysts ≤4 mm across	Late or Middle Jurassic(?)
	Sidewinder Volcanics	Volcanic and minor sedimentary rocks originally called "Sidewinder Volcanic Series" by Bowen (1954)	Jurassic
	Dacitic to rhyolitic rocks	Thick, largely unstratified masses of dacitic to rhyolitic rocks	Middle Jurassic
Jsd	Undivided	Mixed rocks similar to units Jsdf and Jsdc	
Jsdf	Fine-grained (crystal-poor) facies	Massive, dark-colored rocks characterized by a microcrystalline groundmass and 10–40 percent phenocrysts, primarily plagioclase, generally ≤3 mm across	
Jsdc	Coarse-grained (crystal-rich) facies	Massive rocks characterized by a microcrystalline groundmass and 40–75 percent phenocrysts ≤5 mm across. Phenocrysts primarily plagioclase; potassium feldspar, quartz, and mafic phenocrysts rare	
Jsdcq	Quartz-rich coarse-grained facies	Similar to unit Jsdc, but with 10–15 percent embayed quartz phenocrysts ≤5 mm across	
Jslr	Laminated rhyolite	Thinly laminated, felsic rock of probable rhyolitic composition	Middle Jurassic(?)
Jscg	Conglomeratic rocks	Dark-brown lithic sandstone containing angular siliceous rock fragments	Middle Jurassic(?)
	Northern sequence	Rocks exposed northwest of Black Mountain Quarry	Early Jurassic
Jsnr	Rhyolite	White to very light gray, microcrystalline rhyolite that contains scattered plagioclase phenocrysts ≤3 mm across	
Jsnl	Laminated volcanic rocks	Very fine grained, thinly laminated, dark-gray rocks containing scattered plagioclase phenocrysts ≤2 mm long	
Jsnq	Quartzose sandstone	Medium- to coarse-grained, massive to laminated, quartzose sandstone that contains minor lithic grains and feldspar	
Jsns	Sandstone and conglomerate	Medium- to coarse-grained grained feldspathic sandstone and conglomerate containing volcanic(?) clasts mostly ≤2 cm across	

Table 1 (continued).

Symbol	Unit	Lithology	Age
	Unnamed sedimentary rocks	Rocks between unit Jsnr of Sidewinder Volcanics and Fairview Valley Formation	Early Jurassic
Jqs	Quartz-rich sandstone	Fine- to medium-grained, quartz-rich sandstone that contains as much as 50 percent volcanogenic (felsic) sand and matrix	
Jch	Calc-hornfels	Massive, light green, very fine grained calcareous hornfels, probably metamorphosed calcareous mudstone	
Jslc	Sandy limestone conglomerate	Conglomerate composed of poorly sorted, light-gray pebbles and cobbles of limestone (marble) in a dark-brown, sandy matrix	
Jvc	Volcanic conglomerate	Dark-brown to greenish-gray, volcaniclastic(?) rocks composed of siliceous (volcanic rock and/or chert?) clasts generally ≤4 cm across in a dense, fine-grained matrix	
	Fairview Valley Formation	Thick sequence of weakly metamorphosed sedimentary rocks named by Bowen (1954)	Early Jurassic
Jfv_5	Unit 5	Massive to very thick bedded limestone-clast conglomerate; clasts range in size from small pebbles to large cobbles and boulders; calcareous matrix contains ≤5 percent quartz sand	
Jfv_4	Unit 4	Gray limestone, brown-weathering calcareous siltstone to fine-grained sandstone, silty limestone, pebbly sandstone, and lenses of limestone conglomerate lithologically similar to that of unit 5	
Jfv_3	Unit 3	Calcareous siltstone to fine-grained sandstone and silty to fine-grained sandy limestone; subordinate limestone, medium- to coarse-grained arkosic sandstone, and pebbly sandstone. Middle part includes numerous conglomerate beds, typically 1–10 m thick, composed primarily of limestone or marble clasts 1–30 cm across in a sandy, calcareous matrix; clasts also include plutonic and volcanic rocks, quartzite, and sandstone	
Jfv_2	Unit 2	Non-calcareous mudstone (argillite) and siltstone that form distinctive banded outcrops, and medium- to coarse-grained arkosic-lithic sandstone and pebbly sandstone	
Jfv_1	Unit 1	Conglomerate and sandstone. Conglomerate largely composed of poorly sorted, angular to subangular pebbles, cobbles, rare boulders in a coarse-grained sandstone matrix; clasts are plutonic and fine-grained siliceous rocks	
℞m	Monzonite	Medium- to coarse-grained monzonite composed of 35–50 percent potassium feldspar, 10–30 percent plagioclase, and 30–40 percent mafic minerals; quartz rare to absent	Middle or Early Triassic
MzPzm	Siliceous marble	Small pod of siliceous marble and calc-silicate rocks within intrusive andesite (Jia)	Mesozoic or Paleozoic
MzPzq	Quartzite	Small outcrop of reddish-brown, fine-grained quartzite that underlies unit Jfv_2 of Fairview Valley Formation	Mesozoic or Paleozoic
Pzmc	Marble and calc-silicate rocks	Light-gray marble and brown calc-silicate rocks, locally interbedded to produce a banded appearance	Paleozoic
Pzm	Marble	Light-colored marble, generally massive but locally thinly laminated	Paleozoic

24

Table 2. Samples used for geochronologic and geochemical analysis, Black Mountain area, San Bernardino County, California.

Sample	Map Unit	Symbol	Latitude (N)	Longitude (W)	Lithologic Description
129	Fairview Valley Formation, unit 3	Jfv3	34 38'18"	117 08'34"	Coarse-grained sandstone to granule conglomerate composed of quartz, feldspar, and lithic grains to 4 mm in diameter. Plagioclase ~40% of rock, potassium feldspar (including microcline) ~25%. Plagioclase largely altered to sericite. Lithic grains include polycrystalline quartz, chert, siltstone, and micritic limestone. Grains are moderately sorted, mostly subangular.
159	Fairview Valley Formation, unit 3	Jfv3	34 37'43"	117 07'03"	Coarse-grained sandstone composed of quartz, feldspar, and polycrystalline quartz. Plagioclase and potassium feldspar each ~30% of rock. Sedimentary texture largely obliterated; most grain boundaries sutured.
178	Fairview Valley Formation, unit 2	Jfv2	34 37'24.2"	117 07'27.0"	Coarse-grained sandstone composed of quartz, feldspar, and lithic grains to 2 mm in diameter. Plagioclase ~70% of rock; almost no potassium feldspar is present. Lithic grains include volcanic rock fragments and polycrystalline quartz. Clastic texture of quartz and feldspar grains is well preserved; surrounding matrix or pseudomatrix could contain altered volcanic grains.
215	Quartz-rich sandstone unit	Jqs	34 38'04"	117 06'51"	Fine- to medium-grained quartzose sandstone. Quartz grains 0.1–0.3 mm in diameter are separated by fine-grained volcanogenic matrix or pseudomatrix that comprises ~50% of rock. Microscopic inspection shows that this interstitial material is composed mostly of volcanic sand grains about the same size as the quartz, but true volcanogenic matrix may be present as well.
840	Sidewinder Volcanics, dacitic to rhyolitic rocks, coarse-grained (crystal-rich) facies	Jsdc	34 38'08.8"	117 08'50.4"	Crystal-rich porphyritic rock composed of ~60% phenocrysts in a cryptocrystalline felsic groundmass. Most phenocrysts are anhedral to subordinate euhedral plagioclase crystals that range from <1 to 4 mm long. Plagioclase generally well preserved, but some is altered. Small (~0.2–0.5 mm) quartz phenocrysts are sparse; one partially resorbed quartz crystal 1.5 mm in diameter was observed. No potassium feldspar phenocrysts identified. Altered biotite phenocrysts common (~10% of rock).
846	Intermediate-composition dike	Jid	34 38'14.4"	117 08'31.0"	Porphyritic rock composed of altered plagioclase phenocrysts as much as 5 mm long (~25% of rock); diffuse mafic clots of uncertain composition as much as 7 mm in diameter (~25%); and fine-grained felsic groundmass (~50%).
935	Quartz porphyry	Jqp	34 37'24.2"	117 06' 34.0"	Porphyritic rock composed of quartz phenocrysts as much as 2 mm in diameter (~25% of rock) in a felsic groundmass. Quartz crystals are light gray, anhedral, not embayed. No other phenocrysts are present.

Table 2 (continued).

Sample	Map Unit	Symbol	Latitude (N)	Longitude (W)	Lithologic Description
949	Quartz monzonite porphyry	Jqmp	34 37'00.4"	117°07'10.4"	Porphyritic rock composed of plagioclase phenocrysts <1 to 9 mm in diameter (~40% of rock); irregular masses of epidote(?) (~15%), rare quartz phenocrysts, and a fine-grained felsic groundmass (~45%). Most plagioclase is mildly sericitized, and some plagioclase crystals have zones of potassium feldspar replacement.
1072	Sidewinder Volcanics, dacitic to rhyolitic rocks, coarse-grained (crystal-rich) facies	Jsdc	34°36'45.0"	117°06'49.2"	Crystal-rich porphyritic rock containing ~50% plagioclase phenocrysts as much as 4 mm long, conspicuous embayed quartz phenocrysts as much 4 mm in diameter, and ~5% mafic phenocrysts in a felsic groundmass. Sample also includes a volcanic(?) lithic clast 10 mm long.
1104	Sidewinder Volcanics, dacitic to rhyolitic rocks, fine-grained (crystal-poor) facies	Jsdf	34°36'41.0"	117°06'24.4"	Fine-grained felsic rock containing ~25% phenocrysts as much as 2 mm in maximum dimension, mostly plagioclase and subordinate quartz.
1250	Intrusive andesite	Jia	34°38'29.5"	117°07'15.0"	Fine-grained rock composed of interlocking plagioclase (~65%), hornblende or augite (~30%), and quartz (~5%) crystals ~0.1–0.5 mm in diameter.
1435	Sidewinder Volcanics, dacitic to rhyolitic rocks, quartz-rich coarse-grained facies	Jsdcq	34°37'58.7"	117°06'07.8"	Crystal-rich porphyritic rock containing abundant plagioclase phenocrysts as much as 2 mm long, subordinate potassium feldspar phenocrysts as much as 4 mm long, and abundant quartz phenocrysts as much as 5 mm in diameter in a fine-grained groundmass.

Table 3. SHRIMP-RG U-Pb zircon data for igneous rocks, Black Mountain area, San Bernardino County, California.

Zircon grain	U (ppm)	Th (ppm)	$^{238}U/^{206}Pb$	error (%)	$^{207}Pb/^{206}Pb$	error (%)	$^{206}Pb*/^{238}U$ age (Ma)	error (Ma)

Sample 840. Sidewinder Volcanics, dacitic to rhyolitic rocks, coarse-grained facies (unit Jsdc). Weighted mean age=164±2 Ma.

840-1	576	482	38.44	0.7	0.0498	2.2	165.5	1.1
840-2	619	537	38.43	0.7	0.0513	2.3	165.2	1.1
840-3	517	407	39.34	0.7	0.0500	2.4	161.7	1.2
840-4	529	366	39.03	0.7	0.0515	2.7	162.6	1.1
840-5	528	400	38.97	0.8	0.0505	2.6	163.1	1.3
840-6	519	626	38.60	0.7	0.0499	2.4	164.8	1.2
840-7	239	263	39.31	1.1	0.0488	3.7	162.0	1.8
840-8	167	154	38.33	1.3	0.0473	5.3	166.5	2.2

Sample 846. Intermediate-composition dike (unit Jid). Weighted mean age=154±2 Ma. [Note: grain 2 excluded from calculation of weighted mean age.]

846-1	60	45	41.14	2.1	0.0509	7.2	154.5	3.3
846-2	60	70	43.38	2.2	0.0454	7.9	147.6	3.2
846-3	81	70	41.33	1.9	0.0458	6.8	154.8	2.9
846-4	75	89	42.18	1.9	0.0529	6.3	150.3	2.9
846-5	91	112	40.85	1.7	0.0567	5.6	154.4	2.7
846-6	147	198	40.83	1.4	0.0515	4.8	155.5	2.2
846-7	66	54	41.35	2.0	0.0504	6.9	153.8	3.1
846-8	93	121	41.14	1.7	0.0505	7.3	154.6	2.6
846-9	77	97	41.47	1.8	0.0525	6.2	153.0	2.9
846-10	95	89	40.97	1.7	0.0518	5.7	154.9	2.6

Sample 949. Quartz monzonite porphyry (unit Jqmp). Weighted mean age=153±3 Ma. [Note: grains 8, 11, and 14 excluded from calculation of weighted mean age]

949-1	92	95	41.49	2.3	0.0483	10.7	153.7	3.7
949-2	120	154	42.13	1.9	0.0471	6.5	151.6	2.8
949-3	56	54	42.04	2.7	0.0588	8.3	149.7	4.1
949-4	61	54	43.81	2.7	0.0503	12.1	145.3	4.0
949-5	117	123	42.50	1.9	0.0528	6.4	149.2	2.9
949-6	94	95	40.29	2.1	0.0498	7.1	157.9	3.3
949-7	102	115	40.00	2.0	0.0533	6.7	158.4	3.3
949-8	109	184	44.32	2.4	0.0520	6.9	143.3	3.4
949-9	91	85	42.28	2.1	0.0536	6.7	149.8	3.1
949-10	92	71	40.58	2.1	0.0494	7.3	156.9	3.4
949-11	80	100	41.39	2.2	0.0528	7.4	153.2	3.5
949-12	110	125	44.53	2.0	0.0514	6.5	142.7	2.8
949-13	83	80	40.64	2.1	0.0553	6.9	155.5	3.3
949-14	84	82	44.45	2.2	0.0527	7.7	142.7	3.2

Table 4. SHRIMP-RG U-Pb data for detrital zircons, Black Mountain area, San Bernardino County, California.

Zircon grain	U (ppm)	Th (ppm)	^{238}U/ ^{206}Pb	error (%)	^{207}Pb/ ^{206}Pb	error (%)	^{206}Pb*/ ^{238}U age (Ma)	error (Ma)	^{207}Pb*/ ^{206}Pb* age (Ma)	error (Ma)	Preferred Age (Ma)	error (Ma)
Sample 129												
Fairview Valley Formation, unit 3 (Jfv3)												
129-1	128	86	3.4204	1.5	0.1027	1.1	1652	21	1660	20	1660	20
129-2	805	315	6.9531	1.2	0.1054	0.6	857	10	1557	33	1557	33
129-3	125	54	4.1729	1.5	0.1032	1.2	1376	19	1583	44	1583	44
129-4	2081	217	3.9755	1.2	0.0908	0.5	1444	16	1412	11	1412	11
129-5	147	67	3.3936	1.4	0.1018	1.0	1663	21	1644	20	1644	20
129-6	130	58	3.6980	1.5	0.1065	1.1	1543	20	1740	20	1740	20
129-7	269	182	4.5560	1.4	0.1100	0.8	1266	16	1650	36	1650	36
129-8	253	220	3.3807	1.3	0.1049	0.8	1671	20	1714	14	1714	14
129-9	724	322	3.5899	1.2	0.1045	0.5	1581	17	1673	11	1673	11
129-10	185	116	3.3877	1.4	0.1029	0.9	1665	20	1660	19	1660	19
129-11	225	150	3.5714	1.4	0.1042	1.2	1589	19	1678	23	1678	23
129-13	273	136	3.3647	1.3	0.1044	0.7	1676	20	1691	14	1691	14
129-14	703	503	7.0984	1.2	0.1178	0.6	833	10	1661	57	1661	57
129-15	193	135	3.4953	1.4	0.1017	0.9	1622	20	1655	16	1655	16
129-16	218	157	3.6560	1.4	0.1146	0.8	1537	19	1675	46	1675	46
129-17	941	218	5.7679	1.3	0.1088	0.5	1017	12	1588	33	1588	33
129-18	235	132	3.4333	1.3	0.1024	0.8	1647	20	1663	15	1663	15
129-19	208	126	3.3729	1.4	0.1032	0.8	1673	20	1679	16	1679	16
129-20	441	193	3.7951	1.3	0.1070	0.6	1506	17	1729	13	1729	13
129-21	185	93	3.4417	1.4	0.1033	0.9	1641	20	1657	21	1657	21
129-22	172	97	3.7514	1.5	0.1044	1.0	1521	20	1679	18	1679	18
129-23	223	287	4.2413	1.4	0.1197	0.8	1344	17	1745	52	1745	52
129-24	960	490	8.4949	1.2	0.1081	1.2	705	8	1510	61	1510	61
129-25	214	113	3.4066	1.4	0.1039	0.9	1658	20	1687	17	1687	17
129-26	825	398	5.2171	0.3	0.1061	0.5	1125	4	1667	14	1667	14
129-27	358	177	3.3160	0.5	0.1067	0.6	1698	7	1739	11	1739	11
129-28	359	163	3.5816	0.5	0.1245	0.5	1554	7	1737	35	1737	35
129-29	1640	649	15.8246	0.4	0.1068	1.7	383	2	1273	71	1273	71
129-30	1733	829	9.9173	0.3	0.1250	0.4	590	2	1362	69	1362	69
129-31	586	338	4.2422	0.4	0.1049	0.5	1361	5	1680	13	1680	13
129-32	477	202	3.5122	0.4	0.1042	0.5	1612	6	1668	12	1668	12
129-34	305	228	3.8330	0.5	0.1168	0.6	1472	7	1703	35	1703	35
129-35	236	131	3.3175	0.6	0.1034	0.7	1697	9	1675	13	1675	13
129-36	129	65	3.3892	0.8	0.1038	0.9	1665	12	1680	19	1680	19
129-37	95	97	3.4768	0.9	0.1537	3.5	1528	17	1632	173	1632	173
129-38	380	154	3.4978	0.5	0.1027	0.6	1620	7	1667	11	1667	11
129-39	282	125	3.2818	0.5	0.1066	0.6	1714	8	1737	12	1737	12
129-40	879	521	3.8303	0.3	0.1072	0.4	1493	4	1725	9	1725	9
129-41	196	173	4.4435	0.7	0.1235	0.8	1277	10	1682	78	1682	78
129-42	164	96	3.4802	0.7	0.1035	0.8	1625	10	1656	20	1656	20
129-44	115	65	3.4196	0.9	0.1046	1.0	1653	12	1705	19	1705	19
129-45	124	59	3.4714	0.8	0.1066	1.0	1630	12	1723	18	1723	18
129-46	560	187	7.2402	0.5	0.0939	1.4	822	4	1245	48	1245	48
129-47	107	79	3.2951	0.9	0.1023	1.0	1707	13	1655	20	1655	20
129-48	316	163	3.3831	0.5	0.1044	0.7	1668	8	1691	14	1691	14

28

Table 4 (continued).

Zircon grain	U (ppm)	Th (ppm)	$^{238}U/$ ^{206}Pb	error (%)	$^{207}Pb/$ ^{206}Pb	error (%)	$^{206}Pb^*/$ ^{238}U age (Ma)	error (Ma)	$^{207}Pb^*/$ $^{206}Pb^*$ age (Ma)	error (Ma)	Preferred Age (Ma)	error (Ma)
129-49	109	57	3.4168	0.9	0.1029	1.0	1653	13	1656	24	1656	24
129-50	508	174	3.3822	0.4	0.1024	0.5	1668	6	1653	10	1653	10
129-51	719	251	4.8532	0.4	0.1024	0.5	1205	4	1627	12	1627	12
129-52	293	144	3.7713	0.5	0.1028	0.7	1514	7	1655	15	1655	15
129-53	153	93	3.3366	0.7	0.1027	0.9	1693	11	1698	20	1698	20

Sample 159
Fairview Valley Formation, unit 3 (Jfv3)

159-1	367	147	3.3536	1.3	0.1059	0.6	1681	19	1715	13	1715	13
159-2	197	58	5.2320	1.4	0.0774	1.2	1128	15	1131	24	1131	24
159-3	203	149	3.4564	1.5	0.1024	0.9	1637	21	1654	18	1654	18
159-4	415	212	3.2549	1.3	0.1060	0.6	1727	19	1728	12	1728	12
159-6	151	52	3.4880	1.4	0.1064	1.0	1620	20	1694	25	1694	25
159-7	219	116	3.2224	1.4	0.1053	0.8	1741	21	1712	15	1712	15
159-8	169	87	3.4806	1.4	0.1069	0.9	1626	20	1731	18	1731	18
159-9	206	86	3.3693	1.4	0.1067	0.8	1675	20	1738	15	1738	15
159-10	1418	104	10.4211	1.2	0.0950	0.5	586	7	1380	28	1380	28
159-11	206	65	5.4479	1.4	0.0752	1.2	1086	14	1060	27	1060	27
159-12	337	152	3.4465	1.3	0.1069	0.7	1641	19	1735	13	1735	13
159-13	649	245	4.3551	1.2	0.1157	0.5	1311	15	1660	41	1660	41
159-14	901	106	8.3874	1.2	0.1209	1.9	707	8	1610	77	1610	77
159-15	1489	101	9.4066	1.2	0.1030	1.7	642	8	1459	58	1459	58
159-16	235	91	5.5068	1.4	0.0755	1.4	1073	14	1022	35	1022	35
159-17	205	95	3.2347	1.4	0.1065	0.8	1735	21	1730	16	1730	16
159-18	407	210	3.1522	1.3	0.1161	0.6	1754	20	1721	33	1721	33
159-19	505	98	4.3292	1.3	0.1059	0.8	1334	15	1667	21	1667	21
159-20	1024	24	9.5087	1.2	0.1112	0.7	629	8	1469	63	1469	63
159-21	234	96	5.4046	1.4	0.0777	1.1	1095	14	1151	23	1151	23
159-22	1527	109	9.3428	1.2	0.1038	0.5	643	8	1380	60	1380	60
159-23	241	92	3.5796	1.3	0.1063	0.8	1586	19	1717	17	1717	17
159-24	350	148	4.0217	1.3	0.1061	0.7	1429	17	1708	16	1708	16
159-25	1481	331	11.7745	1.2	0.0964	1.0	520	6	1370	39	1370	39

Sample 178
Fairview Valley Formation, unit 2 (Jfv2)

178-1	446	281	4.4323	1.3	0.1088	0.6	1305	15	1707	20	1707	20
178-2	445	185	3.2110	1.3	0.1072	0.6	1747	20	1746	10	1746	10
178-3	185	97	3.3178	1.4	0.1034	0.9	1697	21	1675	17	1675	17
178-4	204	144	3.4416	1.4	0.1047	0.9	1638	20	1654	23	1654	23
178-5	790	145	4.0754	1.2	0.1016	0.5	1414	16	1647	9	1647	9
178-6	364	167	4.5795	1.3	0.1064	0.7	1268	15	1677	21	1677	21
178-7	102	110	3.7460	1.5	0.1053	1.3	1523	21	1701	26	1701	26
178-8	207	136	3.3954	1.4	0.1040	0.8	1664	21	1693	15	1693	15
178-9	412	184	3.6484	1.3	0.1050	0.6	1556	18	1656	19	1656	19
178-10	173	81	32.9864	1.8	0.0504	4.0	193	3	345	133	193	3
178-11	240	132	3.3075	1.3	0.1056	0.8	1700	20	1697	18	1697	18
178-12	130	50	33.3779	2.0	0.0509	4.5	193	4	615	238	193	4

Table 4 (continued).

Zircon grain	U (ppm)	Th (ppm)	^{238}U/^{206}Pb	error (%)	^{207}Pb/^{206}Pb	error (%)	^{206}Pb*/^{238}U age (Ma)	error (Ma)	^{207}Pb*/^{206}Pb* age (Ma)	error (Ma)	Preferred Age (Ma)	error (Ma)
178-13	999	232	5.8921	1.2	0.1158	0.6	988	11	1580	53	1580	53
178-14	290	139	7.1210	1.4	0.0949	1.1	846	11	1514	22	1514	22
178-15	203	105	3.4306	1.4	0.1019	0.9	1649	20	1656	16	1656	16
178-16	23	28	3.3033	2.4	0.1058	2.5	1705	36	1728	46	1728	46
178-17	111	46	22.1057	1.9	0.0649	3.6	285	5	771	75	285	5
178-18	306	103	31.9334	1.7	0.0516	2.9	198	3	186	90	198	3
178-19	207	94	3.3308	1.4	0.1034	0.8	1692	20	1686	15	1686	15
178-20	112	89	3.6741	1.5	0.1039	1.2	1552	21	1694	23	1694	23
178-21	215	112	33.1962	1.7	0.0534	3.5	191	3	202	141	191	3
178-22	156	81	3.3616	1.4	0.1028	1.0	1678	21	1665	19	1665	19
178-23	138	89	3.3536	1.4	0.1030	1.0	1682	21	1679	19	1679	19
178-24	306	159	3.3274	1.3	0.1025	0.7	1693	20	1665	14	1665	14
178-25	225	121	3.4393	1.3	0.1041	0.8	1644	20	1684	19	1684	19
178-26	236	147	32.4899	1.8	0.0484	3.4	194	4	-305	249	194	4
178-27	135	57	32.9197	1.9	0.0530	4.4	192	4	193	134	192	4
178-28	1242	149	25.6583	1.3	0.1239	0.7	232	3	1103	182	232	3
178-29	258	96	6.3145	1.4	0.0980	1.1	947	12	1576	20	1576	20
178-30	189	35	31.5753	1.7	0.0586	3.5	196	4	-540	610	196	4

Sample 215
Quartz-rich sandstone unit (Jqs) above Fairview Valley Formation

Zircon grain	U (ppm)	Th (ppm)	^{238}U/^{206}Pb	error (%)	^{207}Pb/^{206}Pb	error (%)	^{206}Pb*/^{238}U age (Ma)	error (Ma)	^{207}Pb*/^{206}Pb* age (Ma)	error (Ma)	Preferred Age (Ma)	error (Ma)
215-1	309	114	3.5699	1.3	0.1036	0.7	1588	18	1652	18	1652	18
215-2	110	94	5.8669	1.6	0.0732	1.8	1013	15	974	40	974	40
215-3	211	147	9.5051	1.5	0.0611	2.0	646	9	681	51	681	51
215-4	53	20	5.5167	2.0	0.0723	2.7	1071	20	930	111	930	111
215-5	59	52	6.0473	1.9	0.0728	2.5	984	17	958	62	958	62
215-6	144	212	1.9258	1.4	0.1868	0.6	2695	31	2710	11	2710	11
215-7	220	28	15.1713	1.5	0.0552	2.3	411	6	420	51	411	6
215-8	273	69	3.5789	1.3	0.0974	0.8	1588	19	1570	15	1570	15
215-9	118	59	4.6053	1.7	0.0832	1.5	1265	19	1249	29	1249	29
215-10	98	36	2.5651	1.5	0.1311	1.0	2121	28	2108	17	2108	17
215-11	423	162	4.5858	1.3	0.0826	0.8	1271	15	1252	15	1252	15
215-12	482	242	3.6865	1.3	0.1062	0.6	1547	18	1729	11	1729	11
215-13	382	179	5.1309	1.3	0.0780	0.9	1147	14	1134	18	1134	18
215-14	24	31	3.9768	2.4	0.0954	2.8	1451	32	1594	69	1594	69
215-15	120	35	6.5784	1.6	0.0739	1.9	911	13	1016	42	1016	42
215-16	303	174	2.5837	1.3	0.1965	0.5	2100	23	2769	10	2769	10
215-17	79	28	4.5773	1.7	0.0811	1.8	1278	19	1286	51	1286	51
215-18	794	210	16.4477	1.3	0.0542	1.3	380	5	375	32	380	5
215-19	93	44	2.6277	1.6	0.1242	1.9	2075	28	1995	37	1995	37
215-20	709	447	36.9919	1.4	0.0507	2.0	172	2	180	59	172	2
215-21	245	83	3.1488	1.3	0.1088	0.7	1776	21	1766	14	1766	14
215-22	323	202	5.7250	1.3	0.0736	1.0	1037	13	1001	23	1001	23
215-23	52	21	5.2053	1.9	0.0742	2.5	1131	20	1011	57	1011	57
215-24	222	207	5.9656	1.4	0.0726	1.5	997	13	959	34	959	34
215-25	99	182	33.9262	2.3	0.0523	5.6	185	4	-242	274	185	4

Table 5. Chemical analyses of volcanic and intrusive rocks, Black Mountain area, San Bernardino County, California. [X-ray fluorescence analyses. All iron assigned to Fe_2O_3.]

Sample	840	935	949	1072	1104	1250	1435
Map Unit	Jsdc	Jqp	Jqmp	Jsdc	Jsdf	Jia	Jsdcq
Major Element Oxides (weight percent)							
SiO_2	64.27	77.39	67.70	64.88	70.32	57.03	65.83
TiO_2	0.64	0.13	0.48	0.62	0.47	0.77	0.52
Al_2O_3	16.64	11.62	15.72	16.67	15.09	16.37	15.44
Fe_2O_3*	4.90	0.83	3.19	4.84	2.18	6.38	4.26
MnO	0.12	0.02	0.06	0.06	0.06	0.12	0.10
MgO	1.23	0.00	0.80	0.80	0.44	3.71	0.87
CaO	3.14	0.22	2.42	2.94	1.90	6.71	3.02
Na_2O	3.56	2.74	4.00	4.02	3.47	3.21	3.17
K_2O	3.73	5.00	3.71	3.87	4.36	2.13	4.75
P_2O_5	0.20	0.02	0.22	0.21	0.09	0.20	0.15
Total	98.43	97.97	98.30	98.91	98.38	96.63	98.11
Selected Trace Elements (parts per million)							
Zn	56	12	44	122	45	81	50
Rb	121	170	100	129	99	60	165
Sr	449	23	366	442	329	422	288
Y	50	72	43	49	50	35	65
Zr	278	121	292	259	350	217	293
Ba	1174	95	1098	1132	1657	771	1056

www.ingramcontent.com/pod-product-compliance
Lightning Source LLC
Chambersburg PA
CBHW080351290526
45791CB00009BA/2828